THE STOA OF ATTALOS II IN ATHENS

THE AMERICAN SCHOOL OF CLASSICAL STUDIES AT ATHENS

PRINCETON : NEW JERSEY : MCMXCII

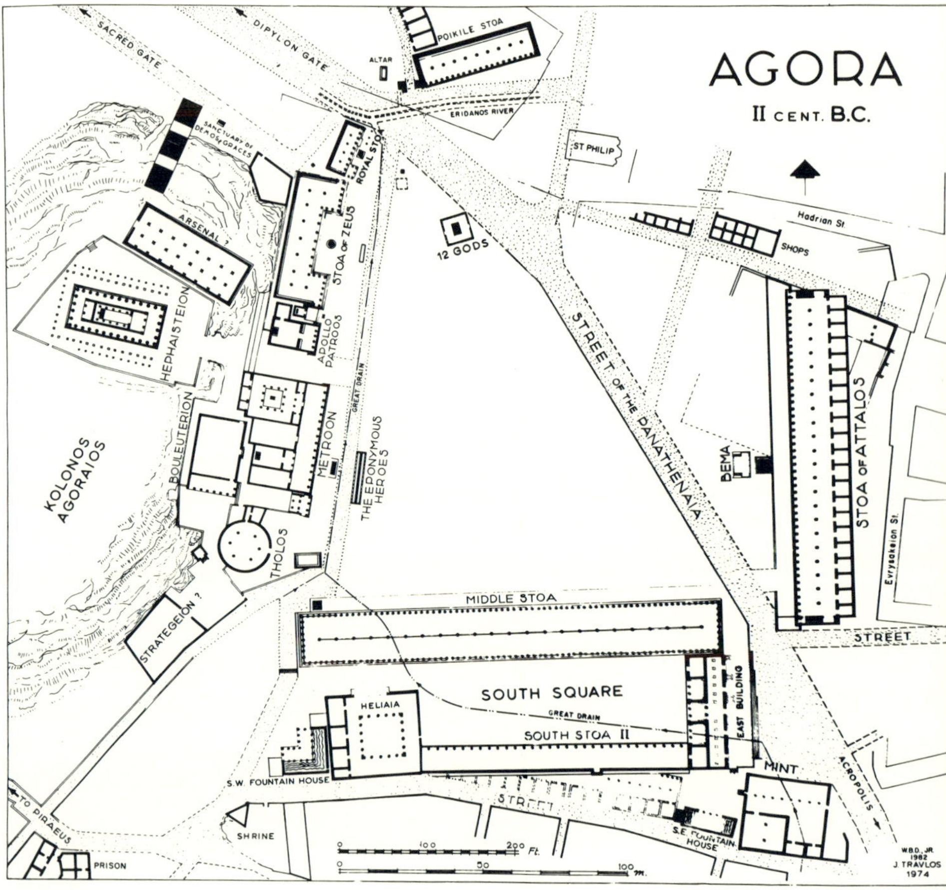
AGORA
II CENT. B.C.
SACRED GATE
DIPYLON GATE
POIKILE STOA
ALTAR
ERIDANOS RIVER
ST PHILIP
SANCTUARY OF DEMOS & GRACES
ROYAL STOA
ARSENAL ?
STOA OF ZEUS
12 GODS
Hadrian St.
SHOPS
HEPHAISTEION
APOLLO PATROOS
STREET OF THE PANATHENAIA
GREAT DRAIN
METROON
THE EPONYMOUS HEROES
BOULEUTERION
KOLONOS AGORAIOS
BEMA
STOA OF ATTALOS
Evrysakeion St.
THOLOS
STRATEGEION ?
MIDDLE STOA
STREET
SOUTH SQUARE
EAST BUILDING
HELIAIA
GREAT DRAIN
SOUTH STOA II
S.W. FOUNTAIN HOUSE
MINT
ACROPOLIS
TO PIRAEUS
STREET
SHRINE
S.E. FOUNTAIN HOUSE
PRISON
0 100 200 Ft.
0 50 100 m.
W.B.D. JR. 1962
J. TRAVLOS 1974

THE STOA OF ATTALOS II IN ATHENS

The long, shed-like building which the Greeks called a 'stoa' and the Romans a 'porticus' consisted in its simplest form of a roof supported by solid walls at the back and ends and by a row of columns in front. Such a structure, involving a minimum of outlay, provided shelter against rain and sun while permitting the movement of air so welcome in summer.

Admirably suited as it was to the Mediterranean climate and way of life, the stoa type had a long history in classical lands. Stoas were used freely around the courtyards of Mycenaean palaces. The type was revived after the Greek Dark Ages with the rebirth of monumental architecture in the seventh century B.C. Thereafter the design was developed and elaborated throughout the Classical Period, reaching a climax in the second century B.C. Taken over and adapted by the Romans, it was passed on by them to serve the needs of the early Christian church.

The primary function of the stoa was to provide shelter for large numbers of people. Stoas were commonly found in sanctuaries and market places, as also in the neighborhood of unroofed theatres and stadia. They naturally became the principal setting for social intercourse in the Greek city. Here, too, the philosophers, being sure of an audience, did much of their teaching. Public bodies such as councils and law courts occasionally met in stoas, and we hear of public banquets being served in their shelter.

The stoa with which we are here particularly concerned took its name from its donor, Attalos II, King of Pergamon 159–138 B.C. Veneration for the city of Athens ran in Attalos' family, his elder brother and his father having already made substantial benefactions.

Attalos' building, which rose on the east side of the Agora or market place of Athens, was but one element in a comprehensive program for the modernization of the old square. Closely contemporary are the Middle, East and South Stoas, as well as the Metroon or Sanctuary of the Mother of the Gods. Much older stoas already bordered other sides of the square. The Painted Stoa of about 460 B.C., the birthplace of Stoic philosophy, closed much of the north side. Discovered in 1981, the building is still (1992) to be fully excavated. At the north end of the west side stood the miniature Royal Stoa, also of the first half of the 5th century, where the Royal Archon had his seat and the 'Laws of Solon' were displayed. Just to the south rose the Stoa of Zeus Eleutherios, a curious hybrid of temple and stoa, erected in the late 5th century B.C. and much frequented by Sokrates.

With the additions of the second century B.C. the Agora was virtually surrounded by porches so that the citizens might choose for their promenades between sun and shade as the season, the time of day or weather prompted.

The Stoa of Attalos was the most splendid of all these buildings. In its great scale, in the depth of its two-aisled colonnades, in the number of its closed rooms, in the use of two rather than the normal one storey and in the beauty of its marble façade this building is an outstanding example of the fully developed stoa. It served a variety of purposes. The spacious colonnades were used as promenades. The forty-two closed rooms behind served as shops. On festival days thousands of citizens standing on the two floors of the Stoa and on its terrace commanded a perfect view of the processions that passed on the Street of the Panathenaia.

The Stoa stood, with minor alterations, from about 150 B.C. until the year 267 A.D. when its woodwork was burned, like that of most buildings of the Agora, by the barbarian Herulians. Soon thereafter the remains of the building were incorporated by the Athenians in a new set of fortifications which remained in use for at least a thousand years.

The ruins of the Stoa were cleared and identified through the efforts of the Greek Archaeological Society in 1859–62 and 1898–1902. The exploration was completed by the American School of Classical Studies in the course of its excavation of the Agora begun in 1931.

The Stoa was rebuilt in the years 1953–56 by the American School primarily for the purpose of housing and displaying the 'finds' from the Agora excavation. The reconstruction was carried out under the authority of the Department of Restorations in the Greek Ministry of Education. The cost was met by contributions from American donors, half the amount being given by Mr. John D. Rockefeller, Jr. The original design of the building was recovered by the Architect of the School's Excavations, John Travlos, while the work of reconstruction was supervised by the New York firm of W. Stuart Thompson and Phelps Barnum. George Biris of Athens acted as Consulting Engineer.

The reconstruction stands on the original foundations and incorporates as much as practicable of the ancient materials. As in the original building, the walls are of limestone from Piraeus; the façade, the columns and interior trim are of marble from Mt. Pentelikon, and the roof tiles have been shaped from the clay beds of Attica. The timber was imported, and this too was probably true of the original.

1. THE CENTER OF ATHENS. VIEW TOWARD THE NORTHEAST (1956). On the right the Areopagus (Mars' Hill) and the Acropolis, on the extreme left the Temple of Hephaistos ('Theseum'), in the distance Mt. Lykabettos. In the middle ground lay the Agora, the principal square of the ancient city. The distant side of the square was closed by the Stoa of Attalos. In ancient as in modern times this spot lay in the heart of the city.

2. THE RUINS OF THE STOA. VIEW TOWARD THE SOUTHEAST (1952). The foundations were preserved over the whole length of the building, and its walls still stood to their full height at two points. Exploration beneath the level of the Stoa revealed remains of three earlier public buildings and many graves of the fifteenth to the tenth century B.C.

3. THE STOA AS REBUILT, THE ACROPOLIS IN THE BACKGROUND (1959). The floor of the square in front of the Stoa sloped gently down from south to north. The marbles at the foot of the Stoa terrace wall come from monuments that once rose in front of the wall. On the right, between the stacks of marble, the Panathenaic Way leads up toward the Acropolis.

4. OLD AND NEW IN THE FAÇADE OF THE STOA. Toward the south end of the building the ancient marble steps had survived, as also much of the wall and the square corner pier. In the reconstruction of this part of the façade representative pieces of the ancient architectural members were incorporated in the new marble to indicate the evidence on which the reconstruction is based.

5. MODEL OF THE STOA. By inserting a false ceiling above the inner aisle of the upper colonnade the ancient architect achieved a symmetrical effect both inside and outside. Openings in the end walls, arched in the lower storey, rectangular in the upper, facilitated the movement of air.

6. UPPER COLONNADE. The outer capitals are Ionic, richly carved, the inner are an adaptation of the Egyptian palm capital, much favored by the architects of Pergamon. Part of the rear aisle has been screened off to accommodate some of the study collections from the Agora excavations.

7. LOWER COLONNADE. The combination of fluted Doric columns on the outside with smooth Ionic inside gives an agreeable variety. The position and size of the wooden beams were determined from the sockets in the ancient stone work. The sculpture displayed here and in the upper colonnade was all found in the excavation of the Agora.

8. UPPER COLONNADE, NORTH END. Observe the good lighting of the stair well and the simple treatment of the doorways in the shops of this storey.

9. LOWER COLONNADE, NORTH END. The alcove with its marble bench underlies the stair. The use of arch and vault, for which there is indubitable evidence, permitted a wider opening than would have been possible with a lintel. The design of the shop doors was recovered from cuttings in the ancient thresholds and lintels supplemented by the analogy of marble doors found in contemporary tombs. Some of the ancient bronze studs were found in the ruins of the Stoa.

10. NORTH END OF THE STOA IN THE EARLY 19TH CENTURY. (Edward Dodwell, *Views and Descriptions*, London, 1834, pl. 71). This accurate early drawing was of great help in the restoration of the north end of the building since much of the stonework had disappeared in the interval.

11. NORTH END OF THE STOA (1953). The Athens-Piraeus Railway (built 1890–91) corresponds closely in both course and level with an ancient roadway that skirted the north end of the Stoa.

12. BACK WALL OF THE STOA, ANCIENT MASONRY. The masonry is of hard gray limestone from Piraeus resting on foundations of conglomerate stone. The bosses were left to enliven the face of the wall.
(Photo courtesy of the German Archaeological Institute).

13. FOUNDATIONS OF THE STOA TOWARD ITS NORTH END. The foundations throughout were carried down to bedrock, attaining a maximum depth below floor level of 7.85 meters (=25 feet, 9 inches) at the extreme north end. In the late third century A.D., when the Stoa was incorporated in a new city wall, marbles from its façade were re-used to thicken the back wall (right).

14. A DOORWAY TO A SHOP ON THE LOWER FLOOR. The views are taken from inside the shop. The original double doors swung on sockets set in the thresholds; they were secured by a single cross-bar. After the insertion of mezzanine floors during the Roman period the original doors were replaced with lighter hinged doors set at the outer edge of the threshold. The new doors could be secured by as many as five cross-bars as shown by the cuttings in the jambs. On the reveal of the jamb to the left is carved a small figure of Hermes, god of commerce.

15. ANCIENT DORIC FRIEZE BLOCK WITH TRIGLYPHS AND METOPES. The roughly tooled surface is characteristic of the ancient marble work on the Stoa.

16. DORIC COLUMN DRUM FROM THE FAÇADE. Each drum was secured to its neighbor by means of two iron dowels fixed with lead. In the middle of the joint surface is a deep slot for a lifting lewis. The broad fillet between the channels of the Doric column is characteristic of Pergamon where the coarse local stone did not permit sharp edges.

17. MARBLE LION HEADS FROM THE FRONT CORNICE. The heads served as gargoyles to throw the rain water clear of the building. Note the variety in the work of various craftsmen.

18. CARVING COLUMN DRUMS. The blocks as delivered from the quarry were roughly squared. The four corners were then chamfered, and soon the block became a cylinder. All this work was done by hand in the shelter of simple sheds: primitive stoas.

19. CHANNELING A COLUMN OF THE UPPER FRONT ORDER. In this series, in which the shaft was a single piece of marble, the channeling was done before setting. The marble worker's tools have changed little since ancient times.

20. ROOFING. The eaves tiles above the façade were of marble, the rest of terracotta. The design was recovered from fragments found on the site, and the new tiles were made to order in Piraeus.

21. FLOORING. In the north end of the building a few patches of original floor were found: a rough mosaic made of marble chips imbedded in lime mortar. The new floor likewise consists of chips of marble (and some of limestone) rolled into mortar and polished.

22. FLUTING A DORIC COLUMN. In keeping with ancient practice the lower front columns, each consisting of three drums and a capital, were channeled after erection. In this way the lines could be carried through with complete precision. Here, as commonly in the Hellenistic period, the lower third of the shaft was left unchanneled and so was less subject to damage from traffic.

23. ERECTING THE INNER COLUMNS OF THE UPPER FLOOR. Cuttings in the ancient blocks indicate that the original builders, like the modern, had hoisted the heavy members by means of block and tackle. The inner columns of both storeys were left smooth since fluting is ineffective unless the sun can strike across the column.

24. ASSEMBLING THE DORIC ENTABLATURE IN THE LOWER STOREY OF THE FAÇADE. Above the capitals comes the massive lintel or architrave, then the Doric frieze of triglyphs and metopes, and finally the cornice. The blocks were secured to one another by means of metal dowels.

25. THE IONIC ENTABLATURE IN THE FAÇADE OF THE UPPER STOREY. Architrave and frieze are here combined in a single member which will support the upper cornice and the eaves of the roof.

CAPITALS OF THE UPPER STOREY

26. Outer double Ionic

27. Inner palm capital

CAPITALS OF THE LOWER STOREY

28. Outer Doric

29. Inner Ionic

30. LOWER COLONNADE, SOUTH END. Among the many sculptures from the excavation of the Agora now on display in the colonnades is the statue of Apollo Patroos, a work of the fourth century B.C. by Euphranor; it originally stood in the Temple of Apollo on the west side of the Agora.

31. MUSEUM GALLERY. The space of ten of the ancient shops in the lower storey has been thrown into a single gallery in which are displayed representative finds from the Agora excavations illustrating five thousand years of Athenian history.

32. AN ANCIENT SHOP, RESTORED. Several of the shops have been restored to their original form and are used to house special exhibits. In this one, for instance, ancient architectural terracottas are displayed on shelving of a type indicated by the ancient cuttings in the walls.

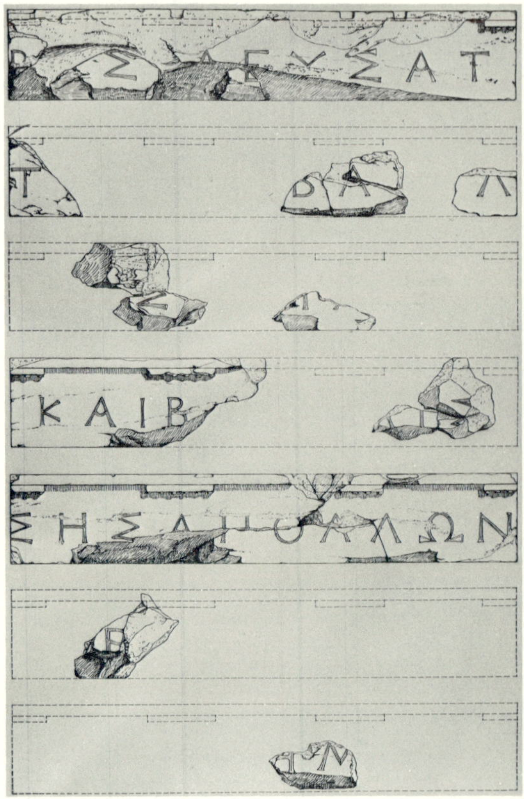

33. INSCRIPTION FROM THE DORIC ARCHITRAVE OF THE FAÇADE. This fragmentary inscription, found in 1861, gives the name of the donor: 'King Attalos, son of King Attalos and of Queen Apollonis . . .' i.e., Attalos II, King of Pergamon, 159–138 B.C. The letters are 14 centimeters (5½ inches) high and were originally painted red. The larger fragments are now exhibited on a pedestal in front of the terrace, the smaller are in storage.

34. BUST OF KARNEADES. From a plaster cast of a (now lost) marble copy of the original bronze (Photo courtesy of The Royal Museum of Fine Arts, Copenhagen).

35. IN HONOR OF A REVERED TEACHER. This marble base, which once held the bronze statue of a seated man, is inscribed: 'Attalos and Ariarathes, of the township of Sypalettos, dedicated (the statue of) Karneades'. The base was found near the Stoa of Attalos and was probably set up in the Stoa as a likely resort of Karneades, the distinguished head of the Academy in the second century B.C. The donors appear to have been young Athenians who were given the names of the rulers of two kingdoms in Asia Minor who were noted as patrons of Athenian culture.

36. THE STOA FROM THE WEST (1957). The Stoa as rebuilt is once again performing one of its principal functions, namely, to provide a monumental screen for the east side of the market square.